Hound Mouth

Barbara Barnes

Dear Becky!
I'm so happy that
we've become poet
friends. Here's to
more readings together!
with love + solidarity
Barbara
xo

First Published in 2022
by Live Canon Poetry Ltd
www.livecanon.co.uk

978-1-909703-54-4

A CIP catalogue record for this book is available from the British Library.

Barbara Barnes was born and raised in Canada, where she began her ongoing career as an actor. In her twenties she moved to London where she is now based. Her poems have appeared in *Poetry London, Butcher's Dog, Ambit, Under the Radar, The Brixton Review of Books, Magma, Poems in Which, Perverse, The Alchemy Spoon* and *South Bank Poetry*, as well as in anthologies including *For the Silent* (Indigo Dreams), *Crooked Jukebox* and *Invitation to Love* (the6ress), and *Cry of the Poor* (Culture Matters). She holds an MA from Newcastle University through the Poetry School, London.

Acknowledgments

Thanks are due to the editors of the following publications in which the following poems appeared.

'Model Railway' – *Butcher's Dog*
'Sorority Snapshot' – *Magma*
'I Am Twenty '– *Ambit*
'High Park Zoo Capybaras Escape!' – *For the Silent* (Indigo Dreams)
'Spit' – *Poetry London*
'Hoodle Doodle Bird' – *South Bank Poetry*
'Capital City' – *South Bank Poetry*
'Miss Scarlett Returns to Tara' – *Under the Radar*
'Warp' – *Brixton Review of Books*
'Will We Become Fish Again?' – *The Alchemy Spoon*
'In 1988 I Go Home For A Visit' – *Under the Radar*
'An Unremarkable Tragic Scene' – *Butcher's Dog*
'Monologues For Young Actresses' – *Troubadour Prize 2016*
'An Early Call' – *Butcher's Dog*
'Mic' – *Perverse, Crooked Jukebox* (the 6ress)
'The Pitch' – *The Alchemy Spoon*

Contents

for all my families

Hound Mouth

I'm the sound of a dancehall fire
rocketing stars into the Toledo night;

everywhere you listen, I've
a song to fill your bucket eyes.

I'm the flood of '37, my glass puckered
up and gorgeous as a Mississippi sunset.

Meet me on the 14th floor of a park bench,
we'll lunch with a pool-shooting monkey.

I rehouse the rhymeless,
paint oranges on their door hinges.

The scent of jasmine haunts
the silver wreath about my face.

Here's a case in point
and I'm skating on it:

once I knocked over the alphabet
and only the lonely picked it up.

Buy me a ticket to space
so I can toast the Titanic

with the first spent bourbon
bottle to rattle through Mars.

I'm more than sodden,
I'm up-trodden and washed down.

Good night sweet pirates of Old Blue,
the current carries my graceful crimes.

Model Railway

Construct a ladder moonwards, then
lay it down across the blank white page
that makes prairie, the ladder now railway.

Tear a boy from the workhouse roll,
call out *John Brown* in thickest Yorkshire,
a scrap of boy with cheek-scar shaped
like a horse's hoof or a father's rage.

Declaring *pauperism is in your blood,*
set the boy in the centre of the snow scene
halfway along the laddery track.
Say *now you are the night shift*
in a roundhouse by the Saskatchewan River.

Walk him past coal pockets and cinder pit
to the turntable, where trains arrive, pause, resume.
Tell him to oil and polish, crank, tighten,
restore the locomotive clank and whirr
that shifts freight and breath across the frozen nowhere.

Now let him meet a Cree girl on 19th Street.
She whispers of sun through jack pine, star-scatter
over Waskesiu, sage grouse dawn dancing.
In song this is called 'sitting pretty place'.
It's minus 40, the moon is hard edged.
Imagine he feels like a rich man.

Queen's Walk Road

My mouth stuffed
with black taffy,
I watch Her

Majesty alight
from the train.
Sheltered by white

birch, tamarac,
jack pine, Her foot-
fall finds fresh tarmac

softened under the Musk-
oka sun. Grasshoppers
thrum their heat

song, as Elizabeth re-
traces *the path of
a Chippewa Princess.*

Climbing back onboard,
She tends to a tingling
near Her left ankle

curve. High above
the Government Dock,
the merest spit of blue

blood swells a belly
aloft on wings finer
than touch. My paper

bag is heavy with Jolly
Ranchers, Jaw Breakers,
Caramel Creams.

Aunt Helen, that night

She pulls up her top to show me the scar,
her breath pitched high and sour from drink,
our kitchen a cocktail of meatloaf and menthols.
My aunt's belly is a ruined balloon pumped
part way to full, as if her body tried to inflate
in a last-ditch attempt to save itself from drowning.
The scar worms a pink path
across the sallow stretch of flesh,
a cruel indifference penned by the surgeon.
It reads rude, a sign-off scrawled at the end
of a heartless break-up letter.
I stare a nine-year-old's horror,
my aunt's face crumples like an empty pack of smokes.
She cries, that angry nose puffed bigger,
mopping up the soak from her eyes.
Her hand fat as a catcher's mitt
raises the last cigarette for a long ugly kiss,
her mouth a worn-out purse snapping round it.
I track the white ash edging away from the red glow
like a high-wire stunt, watch it grow
recklessly, without ballast.

My Mother Smoking

I found you hiding in a box, caught mid-drag
in monochrome, a kitchen table gathering,
your sisters smiling out from their threadbare Toronto life.
There you are, posing, a saucy starlet's night club shot.
All brazen, you stare at me,
Yes, dear Future, I'm smoking. Of course I lied to you,
why look so surprised?
I stare back at the you before there was me,
from my life after you've gone, and I tell you
I think this is your last cigarette.
Tomorrow, at your secretarial best,
you will pause by my father-to-be's drafting board
as an inch of ash falls from his roll up,
and you will fall too,
the plot twisting towards marriage, sons, a daughter.
Truth served up sparingly in the name of love,
you will often tell of the spark that was also my beginning,
of ash scrubbed from my father's white cuffs,
ruinous embers burning crisp holes in ties.
How headline warnings kindled his willpower to stop,
but that no, you never, not one puff –
another bedtime fiction lining the shelves of our smoke-free
suburban bungalow. And I promise I will never,
my talent for deception gleaned from genetics' secret code.
Oh forever mother,
in the heaven where truth has no consequence,
falsehood no sting, I will meet you,
lead you outside, away from the bustle of after-life,
lean close while you light my first, not-first cigarette.
Smoke softening our time-wearied faces
as we inhale, waiting for my daughter to join us.

Silver Heart

Most nice girls had one —
a gift for birthday or Christmas,
before a watch, after dolls,
kept for best in a blue velvet box,
dull and important
like growing up might be.
It daintied my blank chest.
Bored, I would slip it past my lips,
my tongue tracing the outline
of this fancy lozenge;
the embossed front, smooth back,
flipping it over and over,
letting it dangle in the gully
behind my gums,
the cool metallic taint
a taster lesson
in the alchemy of kisses.
When my fingers worked
along the heart's edge
to prise it open
(so I could keep
my tiny yellow grandmother
and half my terrier there,
until I had a lover or twins)
my thumbnail got stuck, ripping
to the quick. Still the catch
wouldn't release and a rage was lit
swift and deep in me.
I bit down hard with my back teeth
leaving two dents visible
only on the smooth side,
marking it forever as mine.

Sorority Snapshot

The front row scooches together,
bends forward, hands on knees,
their formals the colour of petals
or bruises – lilac, peach, dusty rose,
baby blue, shades of fairy tale.
Cleavage peeps over scoops and
gathers, glossy smiles dare the camera
to find fault. Amy, at one end,
turns inwards, her left breast nudged
by Debbie's arm, though neither feels
the tiny pea shape settled in the lobule
by her nipple. She's crouching to hide
her height – like she's rising from a chair
or caught in the moment just before
one is yanked out from under her.

to Marshy Hope

from Truro where the 102 splits
veer right to the 104
right towards New Glasgow
into Pictou County
keep going glance left
at Merigomish Harbour
the sign to the beach
to the thawing Strait
turn to me at French River
drive on to Broadway
past Kenzieville
my hands are lap folded
my fingers layered petals
swerve at Barney's River Station
we swing through a sky of trees
your fingers twitch a St Vitus dance
look at me and think *delicate*
but I'm warning you
I can smell the water meadows
by James River it'll be too late
my kiss is peppery
my long narrow leaves take root
where they touch the earth

I Am Twenty

A rooster's dawn alarm
    in Little Portugal, the all-night
        streetcar staggers in its tracks.

Clouds roll out their loose
    silks, the moon is nothing.
        I lie in wait for your late waking,

the snow a fresh loaf rising
    on the sill. The floor slopes
        away from the walls, the walls

barely meet. I fold into you,
    my arms paperclip the blanket,
        my legs curl to a question mark.

A dream-tear slips from your eye's
    edge, trailing a path to the curve
        of your neck, where my lips rest.

By eight the day will be a bride
    blushing in her gown. By nine
        I will think I have lived a long time.

From *The Heartbreak Hotel*

Mama, I need you here.
Paint seals the window and the clock won't tick.

A letter slid under my door. It read *flense.*
I can't decipher this hunter language.
Where has my flesh gone? Yesterday I was gorgeous with it.

The daylight is wrecked and ugly. It hangs
limp over the lampshade, piles up in corners.
I warn you, the place is such a mess.

I tried to eat cherries from the palm of a beautiful boy.
They stained my lips petal-white. *Bravo!* he cried.
I clapped and my hands fell off. What a freak show.

I'm a liar. I lie like a fortune teller's sigh.
When I say my heart is detached I mean it's on the run,
won't be persuaded home, ignores my commands.

I wait in bed, staring up through my pond eyes.
A steady drip from the ceiling fills them to the brim.

I asked reception to show you the way to my room.
They said you already know.

Marriage

Of course there had been compromise
acts of forgiveness   estimating roughly
she confessed to overspending

at least two dozen times that first year
while Tom admitted overusing
awesome   though this was understandable

his great great uncle having found that word
in 1842   atop snow-laden Cherry Peak
in the Bitterroot Range

Montana spreading out below
stars pinning up the dark
as if the night was just being made

like the time she tried on that dress
straight home from the shop and Tom
discovered what his eyes were for

High Park Zoo Capybaras Escape!

'The Chase Is On, As Bonnie and Clyde Go On the Lam' — *Toronto Star*

You will not find us.
Our dip-dyed russety pelts meld
into autumn's fallen flooring.

Clever jays find us, sparrows too,
our foreheads their sleek settees.
We are not the armed escapees

you hunt for. Our fearsome incisors
drip green as we lunch on
salad selections, our dog's bark

has no bite. Afternoons we are
hippos lolling in the pond,
currents roll our barrel bodies.

Truth be told we loved our un-
natural home; llamas in spitting
distance, the emu opposite

legging it. Doing time we doubled
our years, safe from leopard death.
But who would not roam

if roaming were an option?
Misguided posse, call off the search.
Look for the hole in your fence.

Real Mouse Boy

I didn't know him
or his older brother
hopping and squawking alongside.
Nor had I ever met his mother
pushing the empty buggy through dry leaves.

He crouched on his haunches
front paws wrapped back round
hooking his hind legs, head curled in,
gaze to the ground, as if falling from the buggy
allowed him to be born a second time,

to be born part way through a struggle.
In this cramped position he *scurried?*
No, *skittered?* No, *scrambled?* Not at all.
He inched purposefully along the entire length of the path
unlike any mouse I'd seen before,

but exactly like a mouse determined
to become a boy.
Squeaking with each heave; left, right, left....
His mother a little way ahead. *Is that a mouse I hear?*
Is that my mouse boy?

Amaryllis

In November gloom, I brought you home,
inseparable threesome, bound as you were
in green. I left you on the sill, sightless heads
bowed to the scant sun, as if in prayer,
or a teenage sulk. Dusk fell and your pout
cracked a red stain. I'd seen girls like you
in foreign films – the plain pious daughter
crossing the courtyard under flapping sheets,
sharp cut to the dance hall, camera pans, zooms
tight on flushed cheeks, the technicolour smile.

By moonlight, you began your scarlet unfurling.
Frocks toppling over heads, that easy muscle
of girls moving to heart tempo – the bass beat
as petals surrender one by one into flounce.
From the fiery core of each bellowing skirt
thin yellow arms straining up and out –
the way lovesick fans pulse at the apron
of the stage, the band coming into shape
through smoke. Lead singer tilting the mic
to his parted lips, back-up stoking more heat.
Ready girls. Are you ready? A   one   two   three

Spit

It's stitching your lips, this unsnapped thread, this
moist drawbridge spanning the deep moat.
Its flimsy appearance belies some curious tensile strength.
Such elasticity! A tightrope strung up for a daring stunt,
or perhaps it's the lithe acrobat himself.
Could be a trickster's con or a drainage malfunction,
a low-tech whimsy holding you together.
If severed would your face unhinge, abandoning your jaw
to gravity? Poor clever body! Consider the disappointment
in this single-strand web, for it cannot catch your words.
But then neither can I. What did you ask me, Sir?
I'm a mesmerized zombie, held in a deaf-trance
by the spindly ghoul propping open your crimson grimace.
I know the way I want to kiss you.
With such care, so as not to disturb the sweet infrastructure
of your dear DNA's making. My lips will suction-seal
the opening, my tongue will crawl on its belly,
breach the ivory defences, then stiffen to a spear gum-side,
ballast for the rickety one-slatted gate.
But time is against us. Already this simply drawn line
is weakening under the invasion of breath and light.
If you sigh it could break.
And I will scoop up the remains to keep in a velvet-lined box
or pressed flat between tissue. I might hang a droplet round my neck
on a fine chain, deep-freeze a molecule for future cloning.
I fell pregnant kissing a boy when I was nine.

Hoodle Doodle Bird

back of the Prudential
Mitzi fixes her pouf
waits for her guido
fresh to death, gelled
blowout and nice situation

she knows he smushed
Kim at the Karma
that table flipping hippo
stupid from SoCo
called Mitzi a landmine

but Mitzi's seen her energist
got some love and light
she could wait all day
shiny gun in her purse
baby kicking in her womb

Honest turned up,

gone midnight and frankly
I wasn't in the mood.
Typical. Arriving unannounced
even after I've made it clear
on numerous occasions
that's not ok with me.
Him hobo-attired, me wonderin'
what I'd been thinkin'
way back when.
Said I looked like a condemned man's
dessert of choice. Usual fancy talk,
goofy grin, flashin'
his sweet tooth. Hmmm.
Here's how it went from there:
So...(I kicked it off as always, kicked up the dirt
between us, scuffed up a mini dust storm).
And he's all, *Now don't be like that,* (like what?)
just tell me your worst.
The man dives straight to the bottom,
I'll give him that. *Ok,* I says,
if you have to know it's a bad luck gridlock.
From Money Street to Love Avenue,
and there's no scootin' round back to
Liquor Lane. That's just one big sinkhole,
they've closed off access, left me
dry as a popcorn fart.
He waits some to see if there's more. Fat chance.
Honey, that's not bad luck. Bad luck's
when someone stops to stroke a stray,
it gets spooked, runs out into traffic.
I'm straight in there —
You callin' me a stray?
Hell no sugar, you're the stroker, left behind feelin'
you caused the crash. That's your life's
bitter pill. Ain't nothing can wash it down.

How can truth dress so shabby?
Suppose you think you'll stop me from chokin' then?
He looks straight into me,
my hornet's nest,
says, *I'd just be grateful to rest my head.*
I ponder how long we'd last this time,
if it's worth tryin' to patch things up.
Breeze gusts, clear through the emptiness between us.
He says *needle.*
Then I say *thread.*

I will be a forest herb if you will rub me on your wounds

— *graffiti on a liquor store in Toronto*

This with the last dregs of summer, the drunks by the entrance have landed
splay-legged and awful. Their dogs sandbagged against them
stare weepy-eyed with the heat, the parch of their thick-tongued panting.
The sidewalk is sun-buckled to cracking point, dandelions
stitching the seams, all those ditzy heads wrecked and scattered.

I'm telling you the accumulation; this isn't a blow-by-blow.
It's the headline panic and sub-panics of a scorched August,
continents have shifted leaving us even more ocean apart.

In the northern woodlands, Indian pipe, goldthread, and the palest
shinleaf, administer their potions under the double sky
(green then blue). Later I will step from the shower
into the jazzy rattle of air-con set to high,
my writing finger cooling on a crooked smile in the mirror fog.

Later still, streetlights cast porches into movie sets,
neighbours as carefully arranged extras.
Passersby will wonder how they've been made to look so good.

Gary

We New Years Eve'd in a city folks talk about
saying *I've heard that's a nice place.*

An Arctic blast plunged the temperature to minus 40,
paused to gasp before pushing it further.

The night club was hidden as want, and hotter —
high ceilinged, windowless, worshipful.

We danced and drank and flung off the old year
like dogs drying themselves, then lunged

to the exit. The night air smacked our faces,
turning our cheeks smooth and tough as a rink.

Sweat-damp hair crisped like straw in a blaze,
frost laced our brows, our eyes frozen dry as seeds.

The taxis long gone home, our boots crunched
a hard jazz through the dreaming streets.

Gary I might die now

Our bodies fell onto the bed like stuffed sacks,
the pillow cruel as a rock beneath my bursting head.

We pledged to meet next year in London, then slept.
Outside the spotless prairie drifted and forgot us.

Capital City

I live in a post-war suburb skirting greenbelt fields shaded
mostly in browns. My name could be Kayla or Caitlin, Kyra,
some k-sound. Any rate this is my husband Kyle and our little kid.

Evenings we curl up on the slouchy leather couch, cradling
a bowl of ripple chips, bottles of craft beer. Driving by,
you might comment that we appear zombie-lit by the wide screen.

Weekends we walk the canal path that leads to downtown,
remarking on the season; that dying leaves blaze colour
though moisture is being drawn from them. We can't get over this.

Come winter we skate on that canal, the sun blasting us,
our lips cold-cracked. It's crazy. We feel crazy. When we reach
the Memorial on the Hill we always pause to remember

the Fallen Soldiers and the plaque for the soldier who guarded them.
This stuff is hard to comprehend. Construction cranes bend over
historic buildings the way I'd bend over an old lady to help her up.

Confused birds fly into the reflected sky of the skyscrapers,
Their corpses feather the entrances to the bank towers. This guy
stops to light up, his Keeshond pissing on the Parliament Buildings.

Easter Monday, Toronto

Snow falls again, our beautiful affliction.
It falls on Cloverdale Mall and Six Points Plaza,
on Burnhamthorpe Collegiate and Bowlerama.

It falls on the Islington House Tavern
that was torn down and Pizza Nova
that still delivers. It falls

in our memories and our conversations.
It lines the ditches on Martin Grove, the sills
of picture windows on Cowley, backyard swings,

scrawls endless messages in the streetlights.
It falls with me and without me,
it does not favour, nor would it exclude.

If I stood on the corner of Meadowbank and Keane
it would cloak me in the local fashion, muffle
my wayward vowels. You would think I'd never left.

Miss Scarlett Returns to Tara

She'd clawed the walls of my teen room
days before her legendary escape act.
A red silk flourish. Ta dah! As she fastened
a squished corsage between my legs.
A childish pinprick ritual turned deadly serious.

Endless druggy years, her lousy paraphernalia,
drenched cotton thumbs, thin, leaking mattresses.
I learned her plainspeak: *normal   heavy   regular,*
collected her nicknames: *Aunt Flo Cousin Red Lady Business.*

The horniness of her, slick hot, shiny, a crazy bitch
taking all my best stuff. That raging entitlement.
Nights I curled round her, my tears
siphoning her unsayable sadness.
Come morning she'd get a grip on herself,
we'd crawl into the day.

Hopeless timekeeper, she'd turn up early, late,
keep me waiting, anxious.
The heart-stopping no-shows.
Of course she'd make one final appearance,
track me down years after I'd lost touch, moved on.

Her return shook me, a kick in the night,
a scream through rusty pipes.
The past floods out.

Warp

I think about people in North London
having sex.
This couple sitting opposite, say –
all that wool, ethically sourced.
They pluck at each other,
the train shudders us deep
beneath the riverbed.

I think about their North London house,
the hallway of floppy-tongued footwear,
loose-laced among a slump
of open-jawed rucksacks,
the stacked walls and flat cushions,
the hessian rug they hauled
through India on their ruffian year,
the kitchen floor dusted with droppings
from the mouse who moved in after
the spelt spilt.

I think about their staircase,
mug of old tea, foreign change,
empties abandoned on steps during treks
up to the burgundy bedroom
which I can't not think about:
Vishnu tapestry curling at the damp window,
pointy slippers made wide by feet,
the bed, the slipping spread,
their bamboo dressing gowns.

I wish I could think about you instead,
thickly settled where I left you,
breath steady under our blue sheet,
the skin on your brow re-weaving itself
in the South London night.

Will we become fish again?

We're in departures when you ask this.
On the cusp of thirteen, you hold the answer.
We lock in an airport goodbye,
eyes closed, the important work of moulding
a memory of each other, as around us
others are arranged in clusters, sea creatures
swaying together, voiceless,
the high school dance clinch and slow step
to the tannoy's triple note rise
and reminder to keep personal belongings
with us at all times.
Even so I unwrap you from me, lift your head
from the curve of my neck, and you slip behind
the final screen.
I join the surge to the Underground.
My thoughts are water-walking,
your wings shadow the ocean.
You began as a flicker in my belly.

In 1988 I Go Home For A Visit

You know that pretty what's her name girl who lived at the corner,
you know the one your age whose parents were missionaries in that
you know country with the awful drought in the seventies? Well
you know how when they came back the mother, was she Ruth, anyway
you know she got so sick she never really left the house again, but
you know the dad he kind of just kept on smiling, he was always so
you know tall. Remember he used to put his mug of coffee on the car
you know roof while he scraped the snow off every morning before he
you know left for work? Then that one time he drove away with it still
you know there so of course it slid off a block down, well I ran into him
you know Ted is his name, yesterday at the 7-Eleven because
you know you were coming back just when we'd run out of
you know milk. Meanwhile I hadn't seen him for ages so I said
you know how you doing? Thinking he looked I don't know different, very worn
you know out. Well he told me this daughter, the younger one in your year
you know the Diane one I already said about who you never spoke to after she
you know stole that skinny Trevor boy, the diabetic you
you know liked, remember her with the hair, well turns out
you know she died.

Someone stands by a refrigerator,

who might be her eldest brother
if this is 1968 or '69
he's a teenager opening the fridge door
taking an egg from the moulded tray
if she's there then she's turned ten
there at the kitchen sink
on after supper dish duty
catch! swinging his egg-hand as if to throw
laughing at her air grab
catch! again from this the tender brother
if a third time she will not try
awake now to his bluff
so it might be seen as a kind of dream
this egg she's watching
that lands like a messed-up trick on the floor
its yellow eye loosening towards her feet
on beige lino flecked with gold
like pop art
WHAM! SPLAT!
she's crying crying out for missing
for the breakage and what is wasted
her arms heavy as pendulums
light from the refrigerator as silent witness
that sucked-back kiss of the door as it opened

It's You Girl
for Mary Tyler Moore

I wanted that sunken living room, open plan, the breakfast bar,
Rhoda from upstairs knocking just when life as a single working gal
was too hard, my mascara still holding through tears.
I wanted fake pretty snowfall outside my tall window,
I didn't want anyone to see my bedroom, ever.
I'd selflessly volunteer to man the newsroom on Christmas Eve
because everyone else had spouses and kids to be with,
phone my inconsolable mom and explain, act strong and sad,
scared out of my wits by that noise from the elevator. I wanted
Ted and Mr. Grant and Murray to burst in *Merry Christmas Mary!*
because they couldn't stand the thought of me all by myself.
I wanted Murray. I'd have diabetes, a gruelling shooting schedule,
years of tidy alcoholism, a dignified divorce, heroic rehab.

I want the 70's on repeat, my supper on a tray in front of the TV
before I do a ton of homework, rice meatballs nestling beside peas
boiled to puckering, Mom in the kitchen with her second sherry,
her decisive third, the crunch of Dad's car on the frozen driveway.
I want Murray who will always go home to his wife,
the sped-up credit roll, *love is all around no need to fake it,*
the MTM kitten's roar, *you can never tell why don't you take it,*
that split-second fuzz when I switch it all off.

An Unremarkable Tragic Scene

One day, I will be that woman outside the vet in a black raincoat
like the kind I've been looking for. Far worse than entering the vet
carrying a cage with something wailing inside, is to leave with the wail
inside you, an empty cage swinging at the end of one arm.

Once home, I'll take the raincoat off, leave it on the green chair. No,
I'll keep it on till someone kind arrives, takes it off me. When they've gone,
I'll remember it's designed to fold away. I'll lay it on the table, bend each
sleeve at the shoulder to rest on the narrow chest, double the torso over

along the zippered middle, smoothing as I go. Rolling from the waist
to the neck, all will disappear within the pouch the hood makes of itself.
I'll put the compact packet on a shelf thinking *well that's done,*
have this moment of relief that like a blue pill is tiny yet effective. Magic.

The way the internet makes life appear awesome and awful all at once.
So I'll be the customer who writes a review saying she is very satisfied
with her new foldable black raincoat, but at the same time can't prevent
her mouth from opening on a howl that tumbles into the empty house.

The Flying Girl

How would you describe that morning?
  a glove turned inside out

You were walking your dog?
  as usual – down, across, up, back

A sort of square?
  a damaged square

Where did you first see the girl?
  peripherally
  tiny, on the up

How would you describe the mother?
  a sharp ridge, shabby
  by design not poverty
  fury set in granite

And the girl was flying?
  the girl was crying
  on her scooter
  she was crying for the mother
  to slow down
  the girl was slow on her scooter

Then she flew?
  in a silent movie

How did she fly?
  she was a pink arrow
  the mother a swift and merciless archer

Where did she land?
  in my throat
  i screamed her out
  screamed at the mother

what are you doing you can't throw your

Where were you at that moment?
   on the street corner
   in the middle of myself

The mother was aggressive towards you?
   she was a quiver
   emptying itself
   go away go away you go away go

And so you did go away?

Have you seen the flying girl since?
   mornings my ragged eyes scour the up

And if you find her?
   i'm keeping her
   lodged beneath my breast plate

Incident

Forensics measure sunlight on the pavement, draw
tape from tree to lamp post keeping questions close.

A red carnation creeps from the breast pocket
of the man's city-white shirt,
a gun on the lawn makes the grass greener.

Last night I lay dreaming a breeze,
the tune of the fridge pitched a semi-tone higher.

From the smothering black, the moon
scooped out a navy clock face
on which the quiet woman three doors down

saw the second hand pick up speed,
felt fear as familiar as her husband's key in the door.

The widow goes in to clear up
for Lee Krasner

Because it is what I did

    I do.

   Can I sort us out

           together again

     alone

in your wrecked cathedral?

Midnight drops its black beams

    the floor a mess of you

I kneel down in

    to scrub and shriek.

Death splays its flesh-tones

   your leg hooked impossibly

over her shoulder.

      Where did she carry you

   off to?

I rearrange reds against reds

   we're no strangers to violence.

Dawn is a bleached bruise

I warm myself in

      waking unafraid of this

   high white space.

From the corner a crowd gathers

    they stare.

I collect all their eyes in a row.

Realty

You could be happy here,
refurbished red oak guiding you
room to room, your delight echoing
in the golden yawn of morning sun.
Good windows! Good doors!

Here where Captain John Winslow,
loyalist, settled close to the forks
of the Bear River, not far from Bear Village
and bears, you could be happy, the pillared
porch wrapped around you like a wide grin.

You could sleep in the Captain's heavy bed,
where each of his three wives in turn
turned the drowsy length of her bridle lace
to the midnight waft of the chokecherry tree,
its dark fruit staining girlish dreams crimson.

On the gentle swoop of lawn you could
take shade under the black willow. Here,
three-week-old Grace and all her darling
nameless sisters, long since breathless
beneath their unmarked mound, will pillow you.

Or you could stroll beyond the south drumlin,
follow the boardwalk over the salt marsh,
put in a canoe, your paddle pressing a path
through the river valley, a bright necklace
lifted with every dip of its blade.

Two by Two

At the end they were carried together from the house he'd built,

she lay down first and he curled round her in the space beside.

We divvied up the snapshots, gave the old rooms back their echoes.

I stood where I had grown, watched mosquitoes, black flies

kamikaze into the screen window, the air heavy from another scorcher.

Breath of the evening's lung sucked in and released the curtain

where wild creatures coupled-up across the faded pink folds,

parading to an ark anchored in a waterless sea.

Lion and lioness smooched within the curlicues of their shared mane,

a candelabra of antlers tangled over the heads of a lime green doe and her buck.

Umbrellaed elephants flaunted their buttercup yellows and mauves,

bedaisied cougars slouched through the lazy hazy day,

the twin owls a hoot like the sixties had been.

On deck, side-by-side spiders spun their side-by-side webs,

pairs of eyes blinking from the blackened hold.

I slid them all from the rail, draping four decades over my arm,

left the window open to the stifling night.

Homework

You say go home.
You say be wild, take
your clothes off, dance
alone in your bedroom,
lean paper against the
wall, write standing up.
You say here's *turquoise,*
Paris, broccoli, table, lips,
that's enough, you have
enough. So I'm home
now in my turquoise skin,
pen poised, elbows
propped on the wall table,
the carpet like limp broccoli
under my calloused soles.
Rather, my brain sits on its brain
stem like a bundle of fresh
broccoli, not to mention
there's an abundance of tu-
lips caressing
the room's perimeter.
And you're right,
it is enough.

Except this is London,
not Paris, where the radio
tells me it's snowing.
But here, where sometimes,
November say, or maybe
March and tonight certainly,
the rain, sometimes the rain
is too much. It's not the rain's
fault I unreasonably
long for snow. That
transmutation of memory
from the drench of adulthood

falling back up the hill to
the bright cold lick of childhood.
There, not London not Paris,
flakes flecked the night, settling
heavy, or spun into wind-
pulled peaks. Drifted then stayed.
Snow layering snow to garner
and hold, it could cover me now,
unexpectedly naked as I am.

Acting 101

'We must be able to go somewhere else — where, we don't know.'
— Joseph Chaikin

Find your own space on the floor.
Lie on your back, eyes closed,
arms and legs spread.
You're a starfish. Relax.
I'm going to come around,
ease your head from your shoulders,
cradle it like a bowling ball. Trust me.
Now listen to the sounds in the room:
your neighbour breathing,
air conditioning,
my voice, voices in the hall,
someone running up concrete stairs,
in the room above a chair scrapes,
a door slams, heavy footfall,
someone yelling outside, a car horn,
wind in branches, a gunshot,
shrieking, more shots,
the highway, a siren drowns traffic,
seagulls scream over the lake.
Can you hear waves? Trout tremulating?
Look that up later. What do you hear?
What do you imagine you hear?
At what point did you cross that border?
Next class you will find your animal.

Monologues for Young Actresses

Foolscap taped to the gymnasium door signposts
'Tempest Auditions', lists names of maybe Mirandas,
fresh aspirants to the Community Players Theatre.
In the hushed line-up we practice taming the racket
of our heartbeats with skilless breath control, over-glossed
lips intone mantra-like *I do not know one of my sex,*
no woman's face remember, directed feetward,
like a diver's prayer before falling. Our clammy palms cool
against the breeze block wall, our usual wild prattle checked
by uncrushable ambition; we the teenage toothpicks primed
to prop open the eyes of this drowsy town, the latest wave
of grease paint junkies high on wallops of adrenaline,
our futures awesomely magnified projections on a flimsy scrim.

For weeks my audition piece has subtitled each day's blah
routine, hence I cannot sleep nor eat as the words ribbon
across my mind screen. The bedroom glass has instructed
my hands in the manner of beseeching, my gaze schooled
in Elizabethan innocence. *Trifling* trills on my tongue-tip
like fizzy candy. *Bashful cunning* is a jewel I have turned over
and over in my palm for close examination. I am rehearsed
in weeping, I no longer cry. Sense memories are stockpiled:
prairie blizzards transcribed into catastrophe at sea,
January's whiteout on the highway, a crazy chain
of mauled vehicles – God's tantrum. And as for love,
last Wednesday's spare between Algebra and English Lit,
I rescued the new boy's pen before it skittered beneath lockers,
whereupon our eyes met and found that which they knew not
they had sought. I tell you I almost died.

The gym door consumes the girl ahead of me, I am next.
Out on Main, my dear father keeps the pickup idling
against the chill, tunes into 'Sports Roundup' to pass the time
till I return. His last-minute advice – just be yourself.

An Early Call

Marco is putting my face on.
He rests sure the side
of his hand, pressing lightly
on my cheek a pillow
of his flesh I don't know
the term for.
Ruffle of fist cushion?
I lean into the last
unnamed region of this man,
this stranger sketching brown
to make my brow.
His wrist splays its fan of skin-
webbed bones that clasp
firm onto the row of knuckles,
the part laid against me
being a plump terrain gathered
from his palm.
His fingers freely curl a grip
on the capable brush.
It doesn't matter
what we are talking about.
I am past mid-life
yet no one has held me
this way.

Mic

I stand before you
stripped down to tongue
click and stomach song,
lip smack. Blind serpent
atop your silver stalk,
metallic maestro poised
behind pop shield,
you are all ear.
Your tilted head duffled in foam
beckons. I step a step closer,
you take my breath away.
Germ-laden lollipop kid,
you expose all my insider gossip,
broadcast my morning granche
of throat rubble, air kiss,
and tell the nation, catch
and keep a golden drip
of post-nasal trickle. Scratch track
a molar whistle, a gum cluck,
the slurred fat tip of my t's.
Slip past the dumb danglers
guarding my claggy windslide,
make all my whispers roar
like a broken smoker.
Faithful forensic intimate,
you will detect a death rattle
years before I feel its choke.
I bequeath you all my stuttering
newborn failures, and also
my accomplished consonants.
Go in, scour this dank,
enamel-clad cave, ransack
its contents for sense.
O amplify me.

The Pitch

Thirty-year-old Tess Canyon wants one thing and one thing only: REVENGE. To get this she's going to have some pretty awesomely mind-blowing SEX. Guaranteed this'll be the most erotically incredulous script you've ever READ!

Her sports car, lipstick, satin robe, the buckets of wine she downs, are all red. Tess dyes her minxy red hair an inky black, because in order to wreak revenge she's going undercover, infiltrating the firm that implicated her dad in a sex

scandal, ruining her family. Tess swears on her dad's grave she will have sex with every last executive f***er responsible, shagging her way to the top, redressing the balance of power by becoming CEO – oh most delectable revenge :)

Love, introduced as a red herring, sours the revenge, totally screws up the sex.

Matt Damon in St. Petersburg

Matthew is miserable tonight, stir-crazy in his suite
at the Taleon Imperial. He misses his babes in the Palisades,
his hot civilian wife, the two-week rule has been broken.

Mobile film units clog the Palace Square like a Lego invasion.
Out of rest day boredom, he's scouted the Neva River location
for the crash scene to come, thrown a stone Baltic Sea-ward

in honour of his mother's five eighths Finnish blood,
that centuries-old yearning for America fresh on his face.
The skip, skip, sink, renewed his dread of tomorrow's filming.

Past midnight he aches for the Red Sox, for Ben
before the divorce, Robin before he *ran from a burning house*.
He cancels room service, pops a complimentary grape. Paces.

Should desperation drive him down the hall to my single room,
I'm prepared. I've shuffled the deck, laid the cards on the table.
We'll sit on the floor, my back against the minibar,

he'll have the cushion. There's only so much I can do — I'm just
'CNN Female Reporter 3'. A couple of rounds and lights out,
our call times are brutal. The driver is picking us up before dawn.

My Bad Boyfriend

'I like you. You're a nice monster', *Sweet Bird of Youth*, Tennessee Williams

I teetered on a ledge of my own making,
you were pushy from the start,
promised my name neoned above the title,
the hum of a full house.
My spine rigged with kirby wire, falling was a pretty trick.
I landed centre centre on the pros arch,
my mark a cross of yellow gaffer.

You sat me on the fake stoop of a fake shack
under the fake moon, though the dust bowl
had been real, *and that was the beauty of it all,*
my last line cheated out, silencing the black crackle
of sweet wrappers, rusty coughs.
At the curtain call *bravo* you scrawled superlatives
neat as fishhooks.

I learned to milk a belly laugh from a titter,
was seduced by the magic *if*: what if I were a beggar girl,
a courtesan, what if I burned at the stake?
What if you betrayed me, which you did continually,
praising the one who looked like me, who you preferred
because she wasn't me and powdered a layer less.

Our break-ups were full of false exits.
Costumed in a corset crusty from other women's nerves,
I sipped the air above my lungs.
Night after night you collected my tears in a bucket,
drenched the stage door johnnies with them —
wasteful, but knew that river had no dry bed.
I wore dusty wigs fashioned from my torn-out hair,
raged at you down the prop phone at ungodly hours,
not sure if during notes you'd called me *stridently excessive*

or *excessively strident*, my memory clogged with hack
monologues, impossible blocking, old business.

But you know I'm a trooper, this show will run and run.
We've rehearsed each scene into the ground.
First night cards curl by the mirror's bare bulbs,
roses thirst in their vase.
Ever professional, my heart obeys your tinny command:
Act One beginners to the stage.
Cue rain box, cue thunder sheet.

Bawdy

The rabble is restless –
no curtain can hold their greedy baying.
Nipples fling tassely tears to a stiletto beat
stabbing the opening bar into the floor cloth.
It's showtime, folks!

Seasoned pro, you grab tight a shiny number,
snake your limbs round, shimmy high above
lewd whoops inching you fame-ward.
Woozy headed under lanterns strung out
like hot clouds, you topple into an ocean of grabs
sticky with want. Devotees of the undone,
they stuff your scantily-clad soul with sweaty notes,
strained buttons of resolve pop like candy, zippers
rip at the teeth. Your breath feathers up
through the dry ice dim, your mind floats free.

The velvet falls in a heavy curtsey,
applause clears a path to your dressing room
like wildfire. You act as if
it never happened.

The Smell of Honey

'Interviewer: What's the best piece of advice you've ever been given?
Meryl Streep: From my husband who says start by starting.'

We both know how right he is, Meryl.
Outcomes being unpredictable, to launch is the aim,
to at least achieve lift-off. A bad start still a start.
And for you apparently it always begins with the voice,
your toolkit of clicks, stutters, pursings,
jaw clenched or slack according to an inner tick-tock.
Vowels plumped up or stomped on,
squeezed against harsh consonants or lazing
in the moist furnace behind your trampoline-tight tongue –
that well-trained muscle lying in wait, response ready
for the approach of each parcel of air.
How to move through your lines,
whether breath should pump feeling or feeling crack breath?

But when it came to that famous choice,
the camera pulling in tight on a two-shot, you stood on your mark,
pressing the little girl to your chest as if she were your own.
Sweet scent from her infant-gold hair made damp
by that overly-warm, brown wool coat.
The riddled wail for her real mother who loitered unresponsive
on the other side of the lens.
Later in interviews, you said they were all crying,
all those children rounded up to pretend in the adult dark.
And you thought you had been screaming *No!*
though the rushes showed you silent, the scream turned inside out.
As if there are moments sealed off from language,
exceptional ones but also the commonplace.
Sometimes Meryl, when all I'm doing is opening a jar of honey,
my eyes close and I don't even think to reach for words.

What You've Made of Yourself

A hectic breath forces you from safe wings
out into the bother and bang of flip-up seats
held down by latecomers securing their claim
in the upper circle, back of the stalls.

The slim moon captures and fixes you front,
slicking your upturned gaze, dowsing you
blue-grey. Then comes that crow-cawing jibe
heckling up from your belly pit: *why this?*

why do? Quick slap of a blink and you robot-recite
the opening line, scratched into your brow.
Your voice scandalizes the air, uncorks that feckless
joy of casting away, overturning tables, authoring

mayhem, fanning to razor-hot your conman's skill
for passing off a tawdry heart as glinty jewel
before the thrill-thirsty *they*, who just look at you
look at you look at you having to become a spectacle.

Something About the Limelight

1

it is

neither green nor fruit

it is the night torn open   a white wound

a torch probing the hermit's cave   a wizard's hat

and a dunce cap   it is a phantom lover with a hot embrace

an adrenal spill   it's your fancy man picking you up in his Porsche

the top down   a beckoning ghost   a pushy ghost   a tunnel you can't

hide in   your dealer lighting up in a blacked-out car   it's the white pill

that can swallow you   a sweltering tent in the desert dust   it's the latest

device   playing a soundtrack of coughs and sweet wrappers   a blank page

at midnight   a fat fleck in dark paint   it's the bit nightfall missed out

the pause button on forgotten   your thin pie slice of forever   a bone-dry puddle

stand in it

2

Ching Lau Lauro, Contortionist, steadies the flame towards quicklime,
a beam sears the length of Herne Bay Pier.

The town's upright and curious lean in close
craving the evening's bill, its promise of crude delights.

Legs in a crippling twist, one arm pulls the other through the hole
in his back. Professor Ching is swallowing his own head.

His elastic lips whistle melody of robin, wren, greenfinch,
a fierce dawn sparks and burns through blackness.

Hard lit, Ching's expression is a grim white slick. In the pin-
drop pause he recalls his limbs to their proper position.

The crowd thunders, blinks to find he is Buffo sitting twenty feet up
upon air upon nothing, *To which legion of the spirits of darkness*

does this trickster belong? The sheen of those satin pyjamas visible
from Margate, from Whitstable, from the dim moon, if there is one.

3

from Kate Claxton to her leading man who perished
in the Brooklyn Theatre fire of 1876 during 'The Two Orphans'

Darling H,

You missed your cue – memory's spark.
The pause grew hotter, your untimely dry
fanned panic – I went off script in our sell-out hit,
soliciting calm from the hazy stew that simmered
beyond our bright box;
our boathouse on the banks of the Seine.
There is no danger, the flames are part of the play!
I lay centre stage on my bed of straw.
Red raindrops big as a man's hand
fell from a torn flap of sky,
licking along the border lights.
You were leaning over me, I recovered the scene:
I forbid you to touch me, I will beg no more!

Flood's Alley overflows with the defeated,
melting the snowdrifts. The overcoat you ran back for
hangs on you like a crisp shroud, your face
pieced together in the dressing room mirror.
I wait for you in Washington Street, a blind orphan
costumed in rags – your thin blue flame.
I'm Kate the Fire Jinx crying out for a prompt.
We must cut this act, rework the ending,
danger is everywhere, the theatre consumes us.
I beg you to touch me, then it's your line.
In the silence I burn.

Winter Tour, 1979

We'd been warned about this town —
a fortress built by Bible thumpers
against the threat of nature,
all the countless untamed beasts.

As the evening sun spilt gold
behind the Farmer's Credit Union,
a pick-up truck followed me on Main.
No catcalls, no whooping —

these men knew to keep silent
with something wild in their sights.
They trailed me back to the hotel
where I shared a twin room with Liz.

She'd stopped eating weeks ago
except in the middle of the night
crouched in the closet, nibbling Ritz
from a box. Her young husband

came down from the city, led her
to his car, Liz barely visible
inside her coat that had grown huge
as she'd starved. The winter moon

took Chris and me to the end of town,
at the edge of dark prairie. We shared
a spliff scored off the mayor's son,
the worst punchline of our show

on repeat in my mind — *I left my harp
in Sam Frank's disco.* Next morning
we moved on, freeing the town
of whores, junkies, lunatics.

Meadow Lake

Our show came to an end where the road did.
After months of touring the frozen prairie
we drove due north through a scribble of pines
that gradually became thicker, the way
a bored child fills up the rest of a picture.

The final night lit by a top-of-the-world moon,
we escaped the air too cold and new,
tunnelled through the haze of the hotel bar,
drank lukewarm draft, left before dawn,
hugging off-license red up to our rooms.

The corkscrew slipped in Helen's hand,
skewering her flesh between finger and thumb.
We watched blood and wine mix, purpling
the bedspread. Sleep came to the knocking
of radiators, the jukebox thumping the floor.

June morning sun meant Spring had come
to Meadow Lake. I shed my Goodwill fur, left it
to hang rangy and spent in the closet. Knowing
we could go no further, we turned the van around,
headed back over the thin warm crust of the earth.

Motion Capture

Summer in Nipissing
Milky Way covering up the dark
Lying next to me you say   *poor Ursa Minor*
Nightly cast in a lesser role before a gawping crowd
Little bear stuck still   way upstage
On that black backdrop
So we unpin him
Fasten his seven stars to the soles of your feet
Your hands   belly   chest   forehead
Then you charge through hemlock and spruce
Roar across Lake Temagami
And I'm blinking
Blinking like a stop frame camera
Crazy with fear that I might one day
Forget what you look like

End Notes

'Queen's Walk Road' – The small town of Torrance, Ontario was the only stop in West Muskoka made by Her Majesty Queen Elizabeth II on her tour of Canada in 1959. The community paved and named Queen's Walk Road in her honour. Muskoka is located on the traditional territories of the Anishnabeег and the Wahta Mohawks peoples. The mosquito population is extremely active during the summer months.

'Hoodle Doodle Bird' – This mystical creature is also known as the Jersey Devil. According to widespread legend, the Jersey Devil was birthed by a Mrs Leeds who invoked the devil by saying 'let it be the devil' during the birth of her 13th child. After the baby was born, it transformed into a devil-like creature and flew off to the Pine Barrens in southern New Jersey.

'The widow goes in to clear up' – Lee Krasner was an American abstract expressionist painter. She was married to Jackson Pollock who died in a single car crash while driving with his friend Edith Metzger who also died, and his mistress Ruth Kligman who survived. Afterward, Lee Krasner moved into Pollock's studio in a converted barn, painting on larger canvases than her previous work.

'Realty' – Bear River, Nova Scotia was originally inhabited by the Mi'kmaq. During the American Revolution, many loyalist refugees settled in the area. Captain John Winslow is a figment of my imagination.